HONGXIN
LOSGET

"The Vibrant Future" International Education Project for Young Artists

A Girl in Millions of Colors
Painting, Calligraphy and Photography by Hongxin Song

ARTIST HONGXIN SONG
CHIEF EDITOR YEMEN CHEN
EXECUTIVE COORDINATORS FANGYU REN, XIAOJING HONG, YI SONG, JINGLIN GUO
COVER AND INTERIOR DESIGN BY TIGER HUPO

LOSGET
LOSGET PRESS
2019

The publication of this book is part of a benevolent program - "The Vibrant Future" International Education Project for Young Artists, sponsored by the International Society of Young Artists. All of the earnings from the publication of this book will be donated to improve education for young artists.

Artist: Hongxin Song
Chief Editor: Yemen Chen
Editorial Board: Fangyu Ren, Xiaojing Hong, Yi Song, Jinglin Guo

LOSGET
Copyright © 2019 by Losget Press
All rights reserved.
Published in the United States by Losget Press, Los Angeles
Originally published in Paperback in the United States by Losget Press, in 2019
Names: Song, Hongxin, author.
Title: A Girl in Millions of Colors: Painting, Calligraphy and Photography by Hongxin Song / Hongxin Song.
Description: Second Edition. | Los Angeles: Losget Press, 2019.
Identifiers: ISBN-13: 978-1-7328459-5-4 | ISBN-10: 1-7328459-5-6 | eBookISBN-13: 978-1-7328459-4-7 | eBookISBN-10: 1-7328459-4-8
www.losget.com
E-mail: contact@losget.com
Book design by Tiger Hupo
First Printing. 2019.

PROLOGUE

The paintings, calligraphy, and photography created by Hongxin Song in this book are full of vitality. The artworks showcase her solid artistic skills and astounding creativity. This book includes sketches, pencil drawings, watercolors, oil paintings, and other different forms of art. The bold lines and vibrant colors showcase Hongxin Song's extraordinary talents. Hongxin Song's calligraphy is unique, just like her personality – wild but polite, adventurous yet discreet.

Hongxin Song' mother has been supportive of her education when she was a child. Not only did Song's mother stress the importance of academics, but she also encouraged her involvement in extracurricular activities. Hongxin Song has learned painting, calligraphy, piano, guitar, bamboo flute, tennis, swimming, taekwondo, and self-taught photography. She is a determined perfectionist girl who stops at nothing to make sure she is satisfied with her work. Through the school courses that she enjoys, her innate curiosity shows through her enthusiasm and energy, which always makes her grow rapidly.

During the holidays her mother always takes Hongxin Song to travel around the world. Exploring the legend of Pharaoh, boating in Venice, hearing the stories of Ponte dei Sospiri, going to the Parthenon, learning about the myth of Athena, and looking at the sunrises in the Himalayas has broadened her knowledge and opened her eyes to the endless amount of possibilities.

Despite having numerous hobbies, Hongxin Song's dream has always been to explore the complexities of life as a biologist. When she was in second grade, her mother gifted her a microscope, and since then, her curiosity and passion for biology has blossomed. The microscope opened up a magical world for her and made her fall in love with biology.

In addition to following the old Chinese saying read thousands of books and run thousands of miles, Hongxin Song's mother is very supportive of her contributions in the social welfare activities. When participating in the "Wildness Training and Reintroduction of Giant Panda" at the Giant Panda Base in Wolong Nature Reserve, Hongxin Song cut the bamboo, cleaned the living room, and took care of the wild giant pandas with the team at an altitude of more than 3,000 meters. She also observed their living habits and obtained first-hand bioscience data. Such activities not only further cultivated her love but also expanded her knowledge and strengthened her relationship between animals and nature.

Hongxin Song's personality resembles her artworks as they are not restricted to the tradition as they represent a new vision of the young generation. Her photography, with a glimpse of the world, captures an ordinary and unique moment of light and shadow. In her Hong Kong night scene photography series, the hustle of the crowd and the urgency of the traffic create the timeless portrait of Hong Kong. She also loves to captures flowers from different countries in various shapes, as they are in full bloom, or about to bloom.

Since the beginning of this century, the world has undergone tremendous changes, perhaps only artists like her can adapt to such times. Hongxin Song's photography is not only a visual representation of who she is but also displays a glimpse of the ever-changing world.

Hongxin Song is currently enrolled in University of California, San Diego to study in the field of cognitive science, wish her luck on her journey and all the success that follows.

seeks the tradition
through calligraphy

captures the moment
through photography

sees the future through
painting

CONTENTS

Part 1 Painting 1

Part 2 Calligraphy 25

Part 3 Photography 37

Part 4 Hongxin Song 73

Part 1
PAINTING

Portrait (not original), pencil, 2012

Figure Sketches (not original), pencil, 2012

Copy of Xuan Ai's work, pencil, 2012

Scenery Sketches (not original), pencil, 2014

A Corner of Qingdao Sculpture Park, pencil, 2014

Figure Sketches (not original), pencil, 2014

Anime Sketches (not original), gouache, 2014

Copy of Yuki Midorikawa's work, gouache, 2014

Scenery Sketches (not original), watercolor, 2015

Anime Sketches (not original), charcoal, 2015

Scenery Sketches (not original), watercolor, 2015

Flying, watercolor, 2015

Copy of Van Gogh's work, oil, 2015

Copy of Jennifer Healy's work, watercolor, 2015

A Girl in Millions of Colors

Copy of Geli Gu's work, colored pencil, 2015

Portrait (not original), watercolor, 2015

Copy of Weinian Du's work, watercolor, 2015

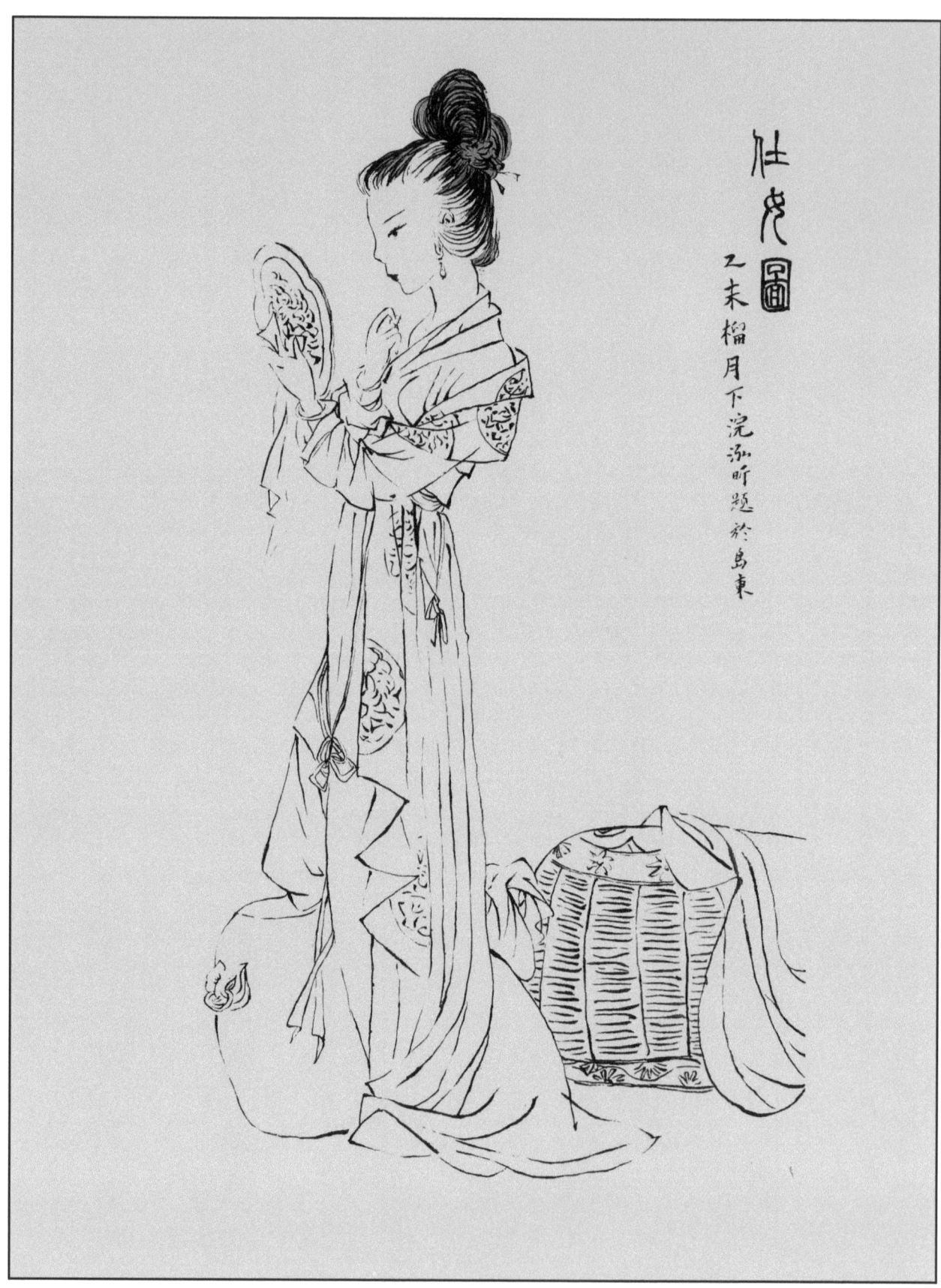

Portrait (not original), Chinese watercolor, 2015

Fashion Design Sketch, watercolor, 2015

Copy of Claude Monet's work, oil, 2015

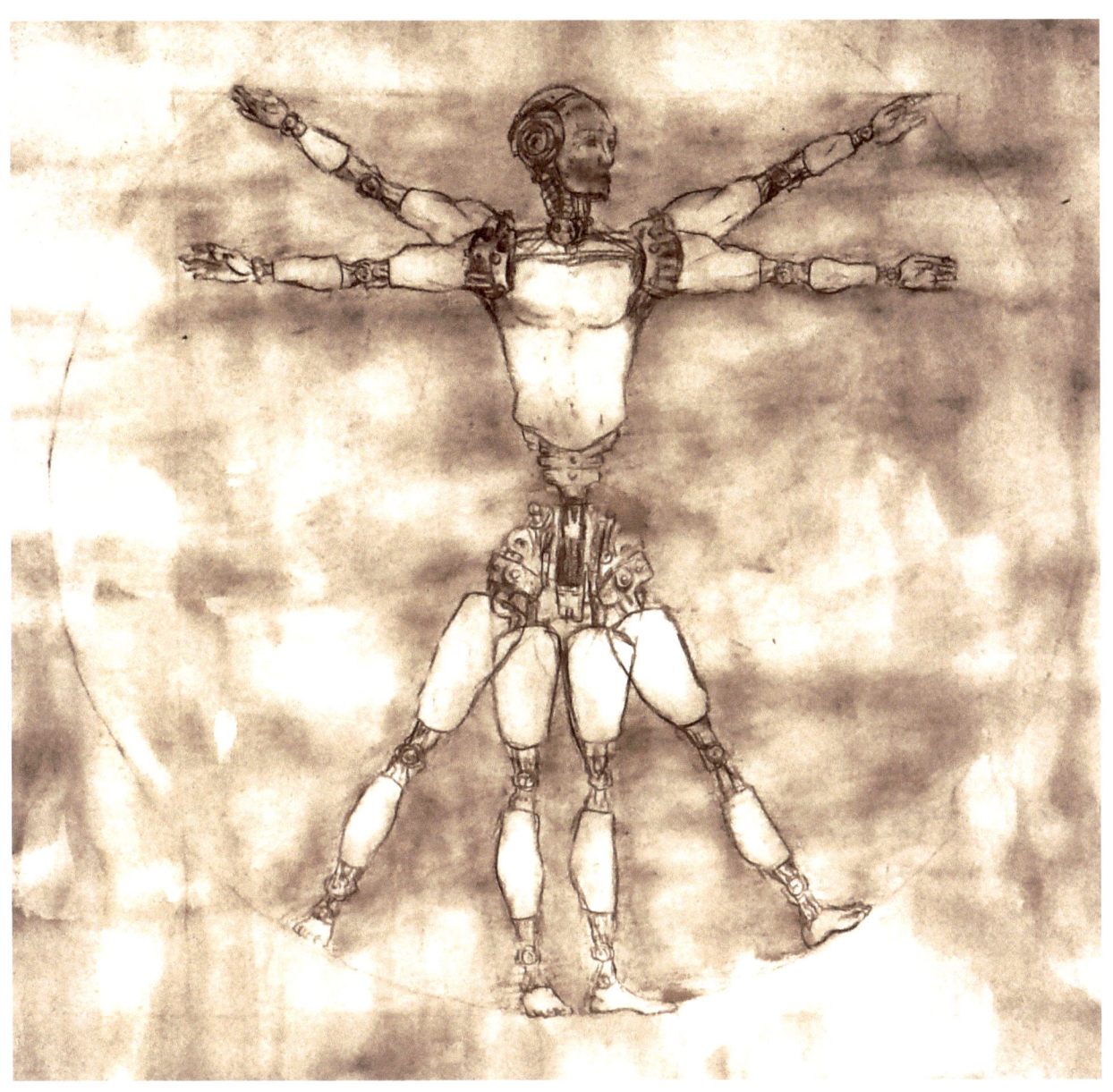

The Robot, gouache, 2015

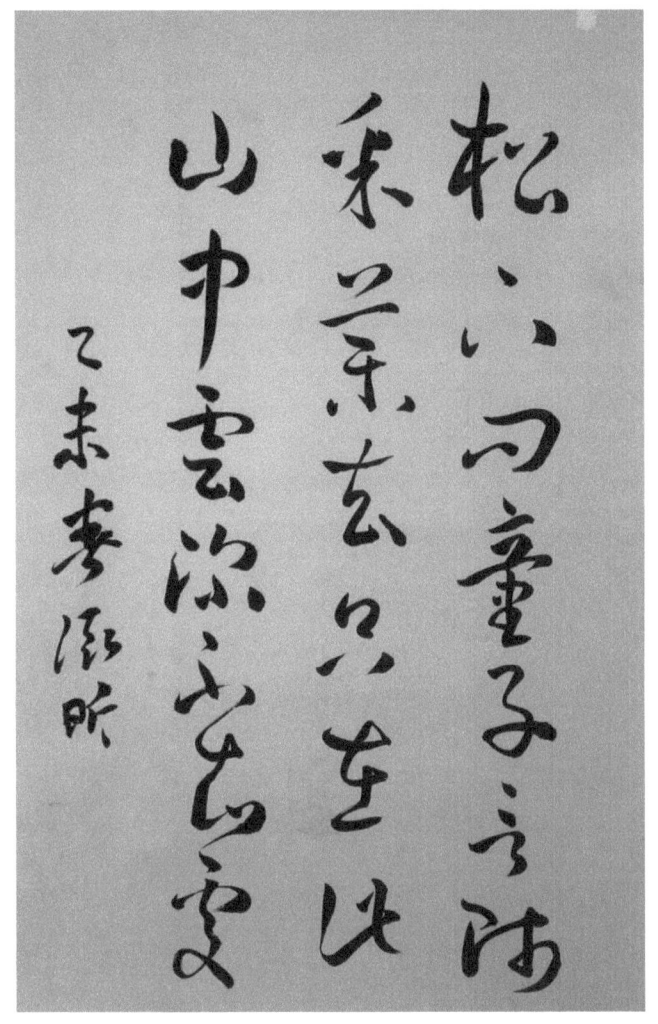

Part 2
CALLIGRAPHY

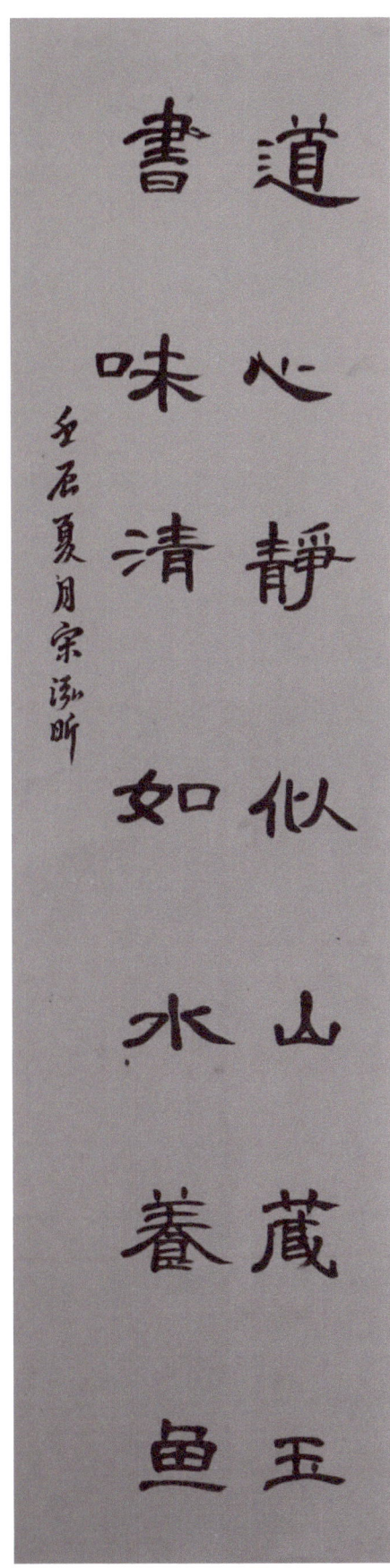
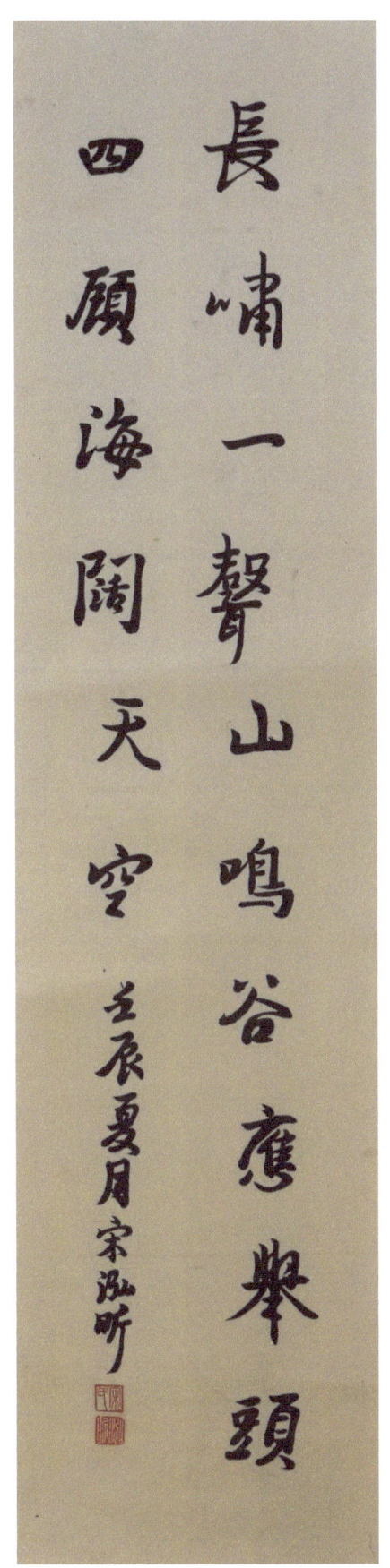

The Couplet, 2012   *The Couplet*, 2012

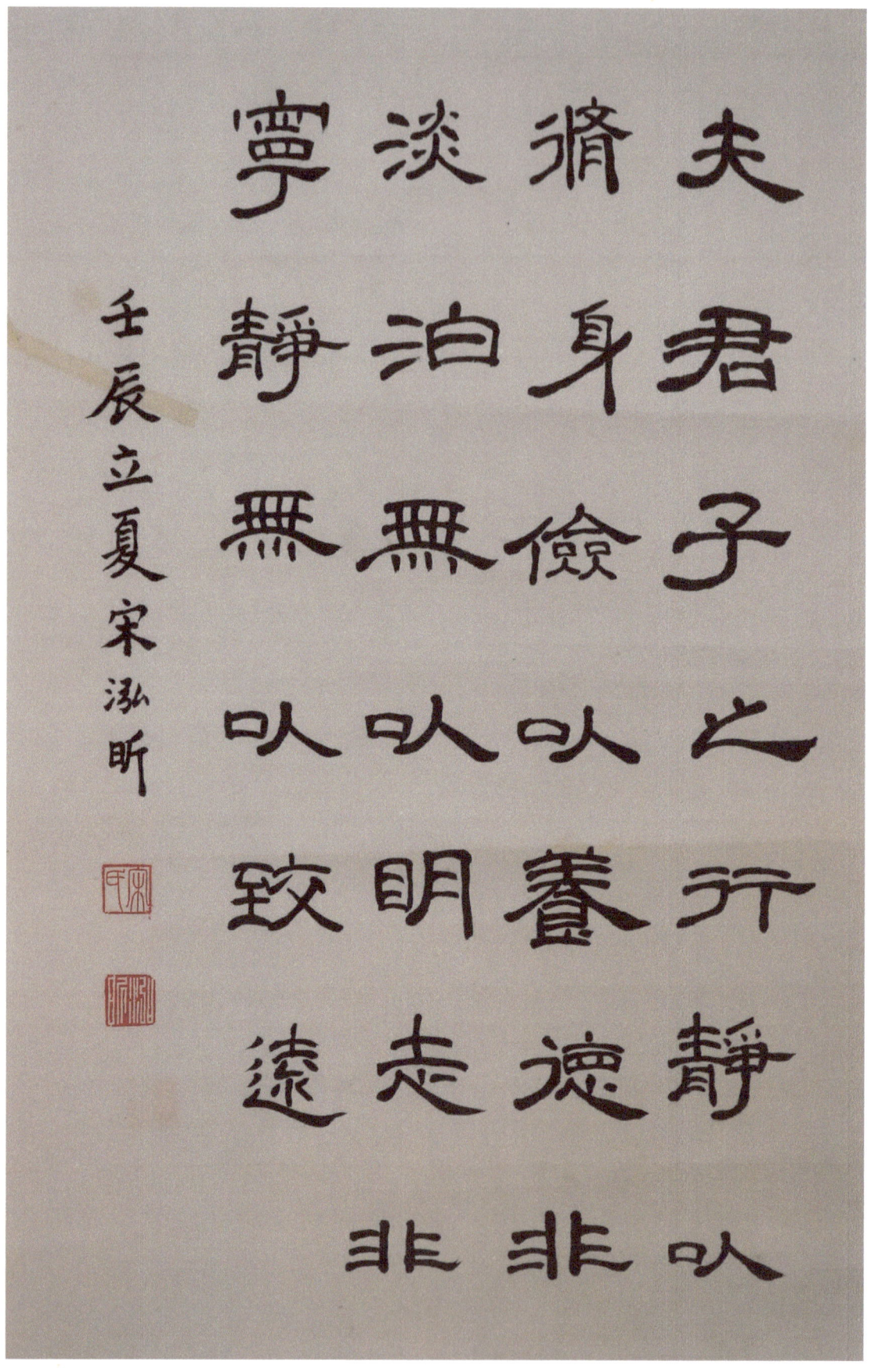

Selection from *Son of the Commandment*, 2012

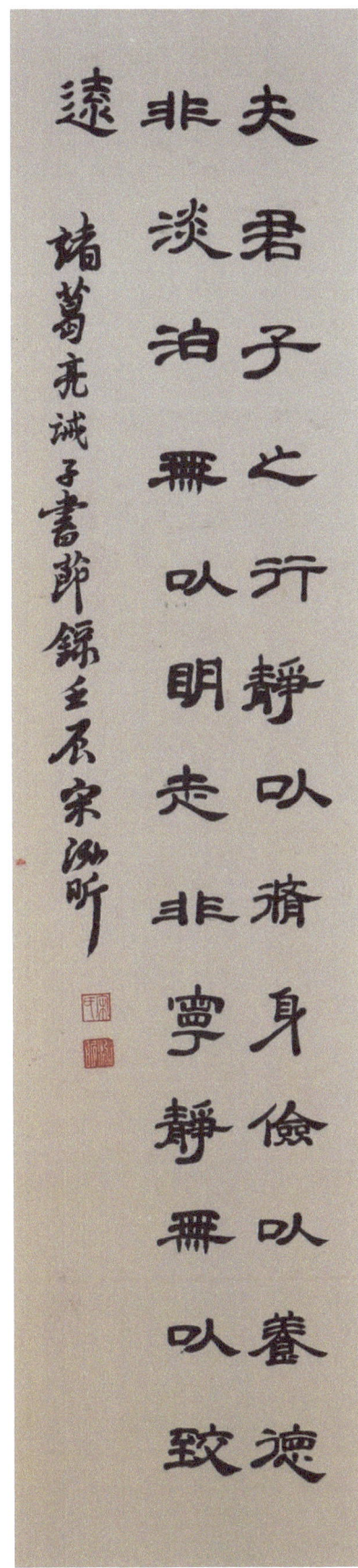

Selection from *Son of the Commandment*, 2012

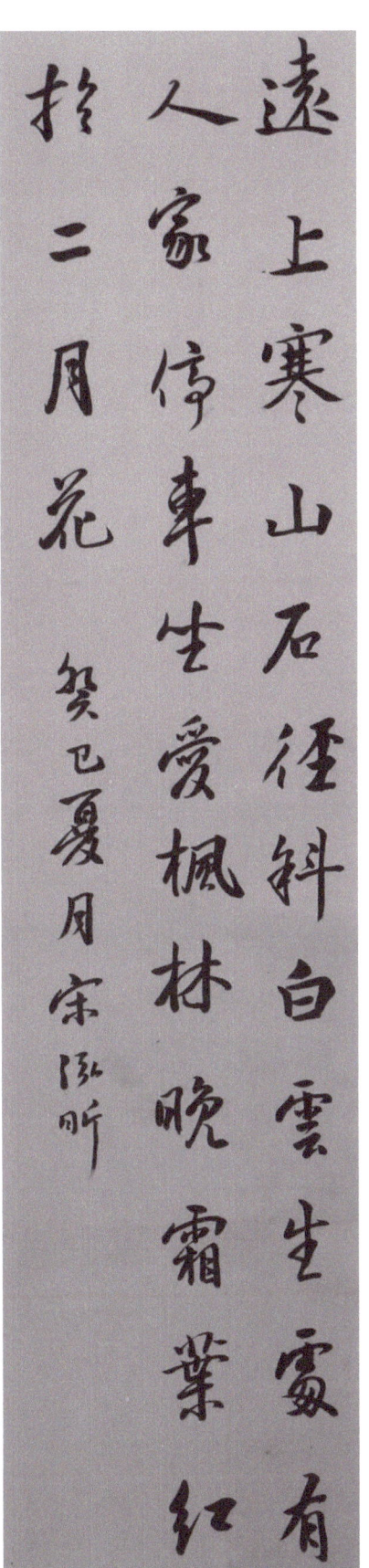

Travelling in the Mountains, 2013

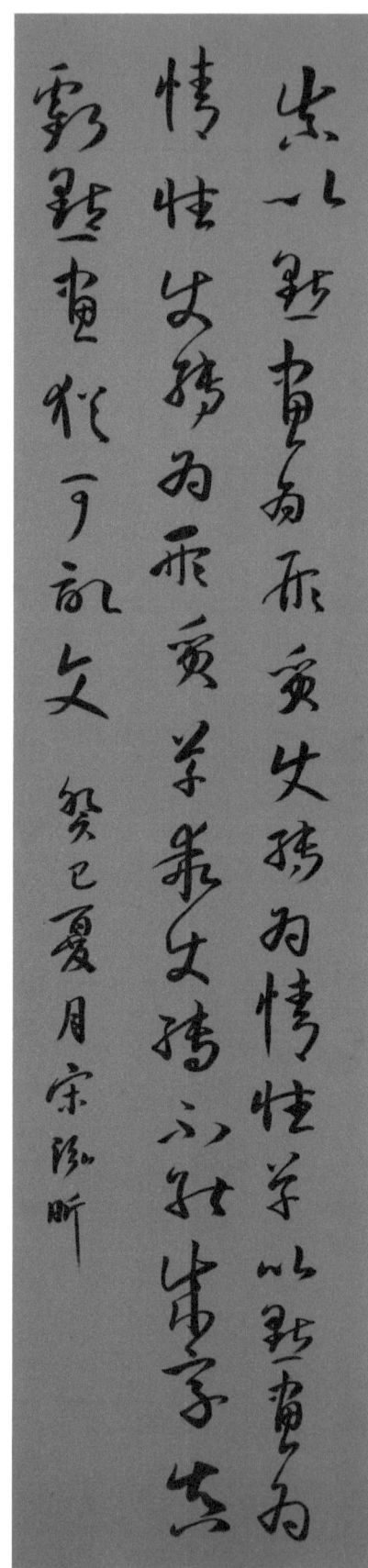

Selection from *A Narrative on Calligraphy*, 2013

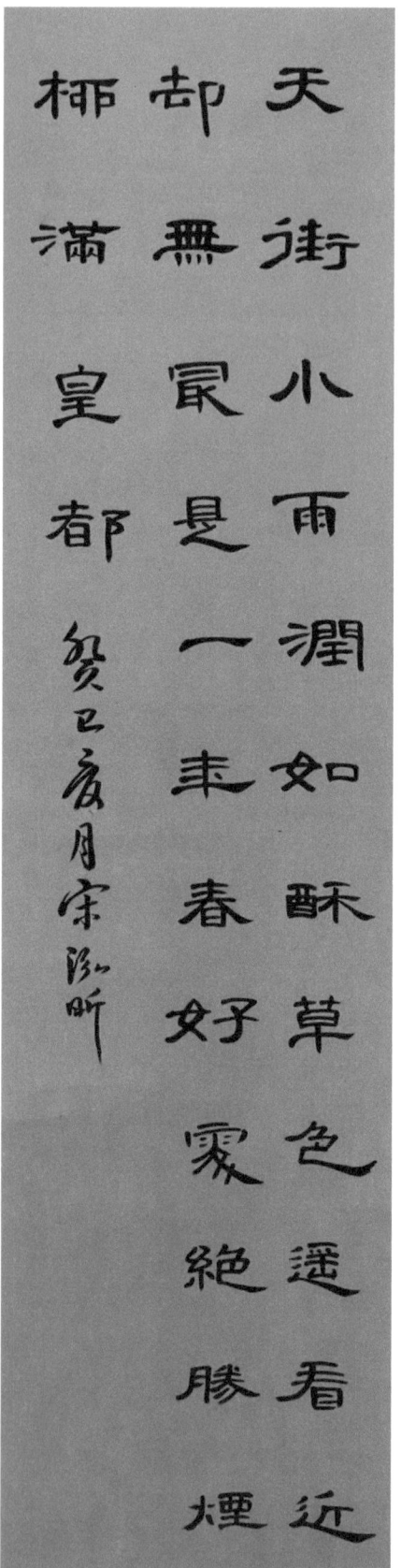

Light Rain in Early Spring, 2013

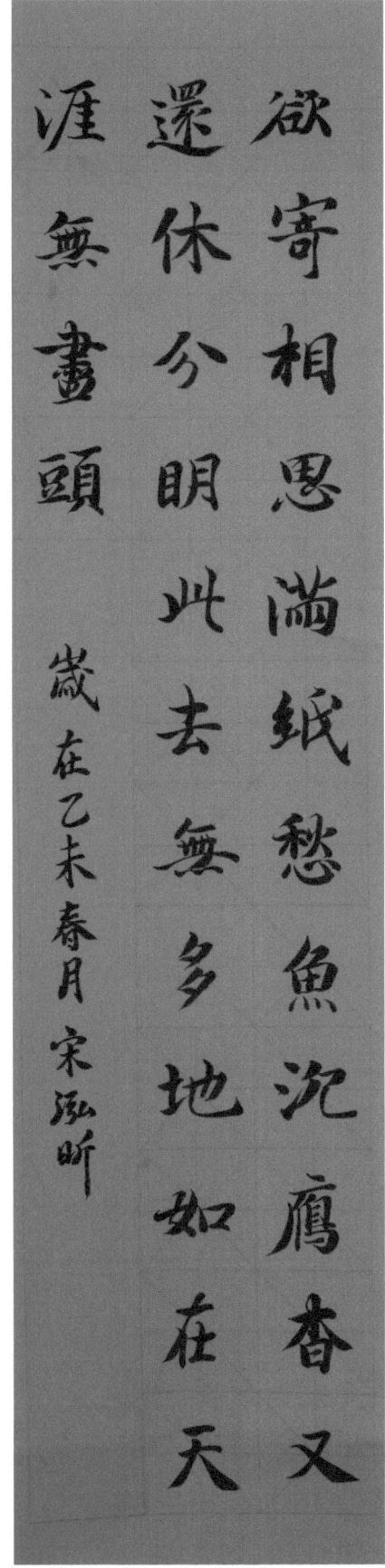

Sending Feelings, 2015

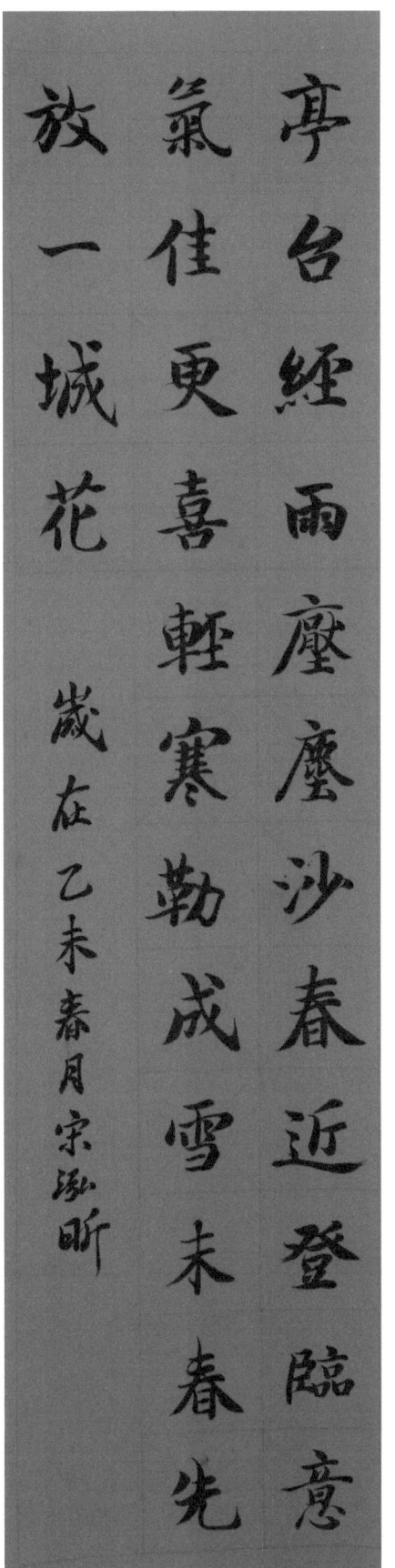

When Spring is Coming, 2015

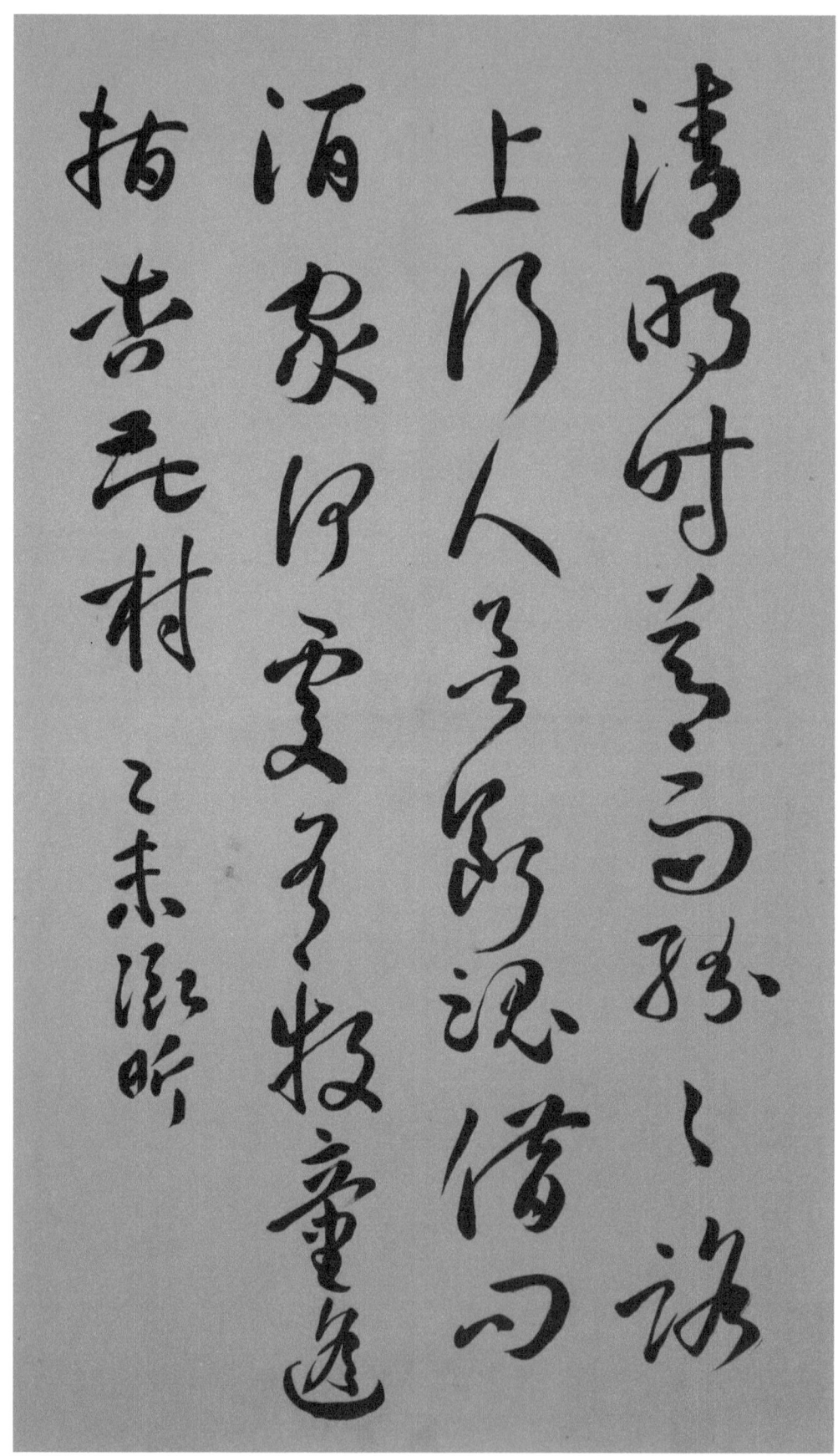

The Tomb Sweeping Day, 2015

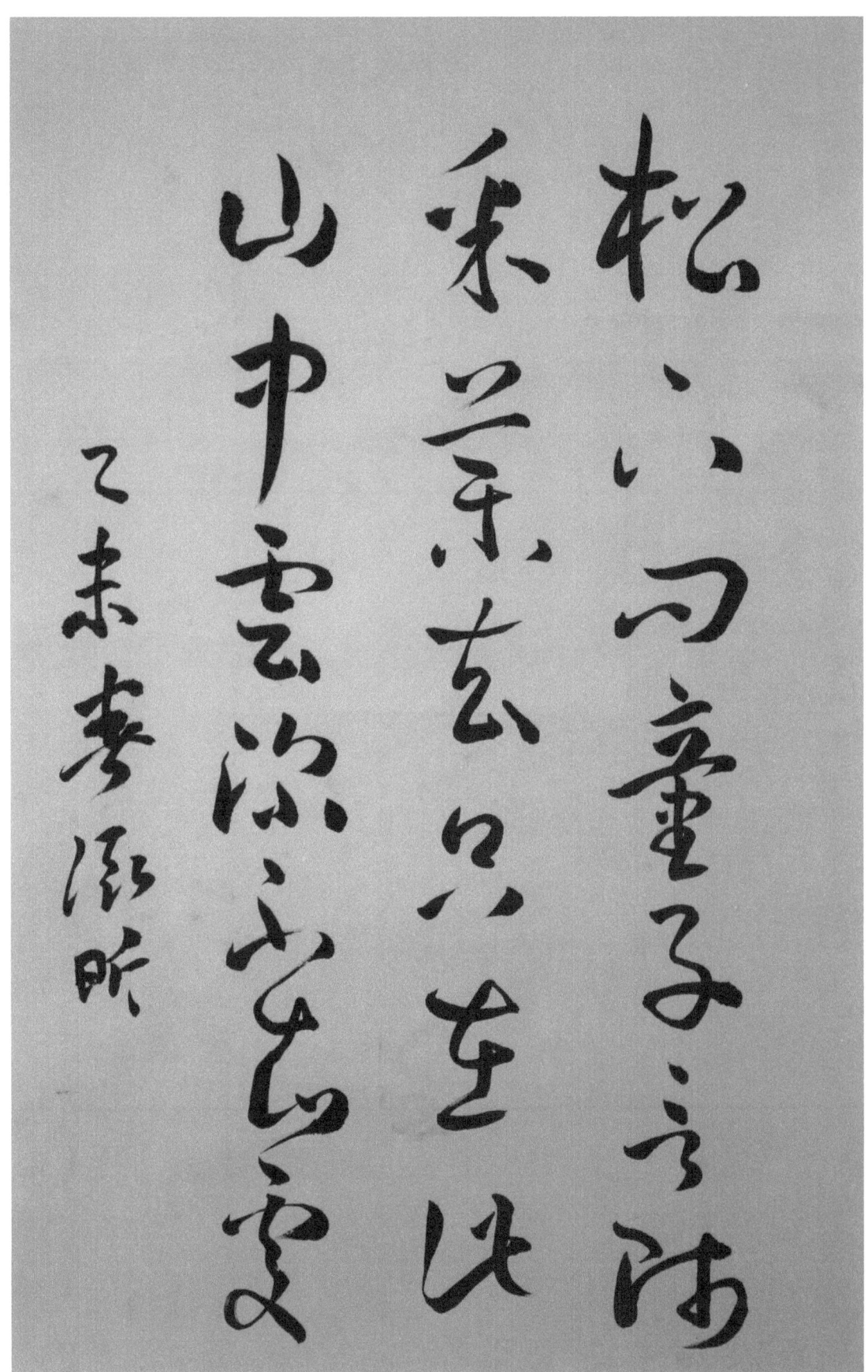

A Note to a Recluse I Missed Out on Seeing, 2015

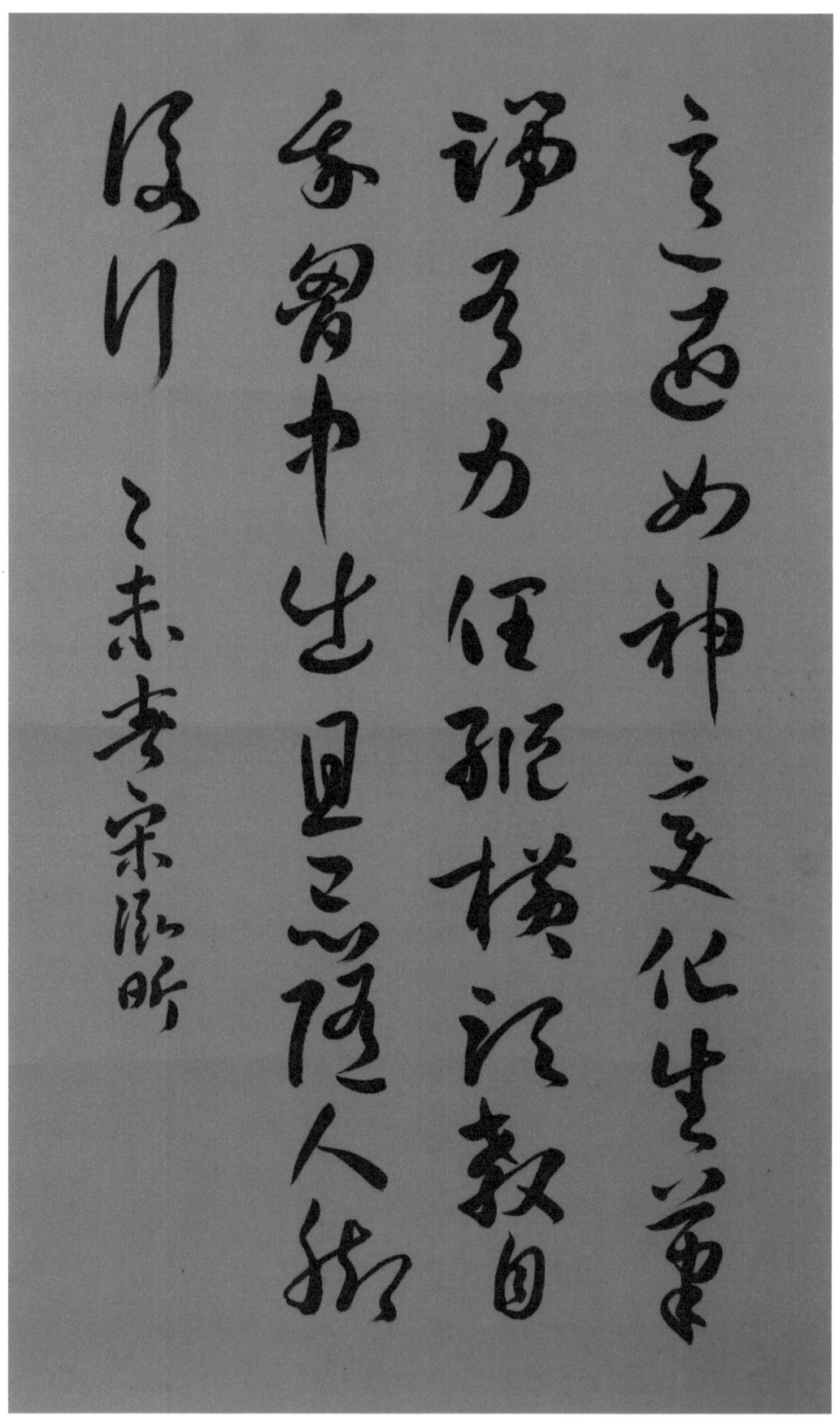

On Poetry (V), 2015

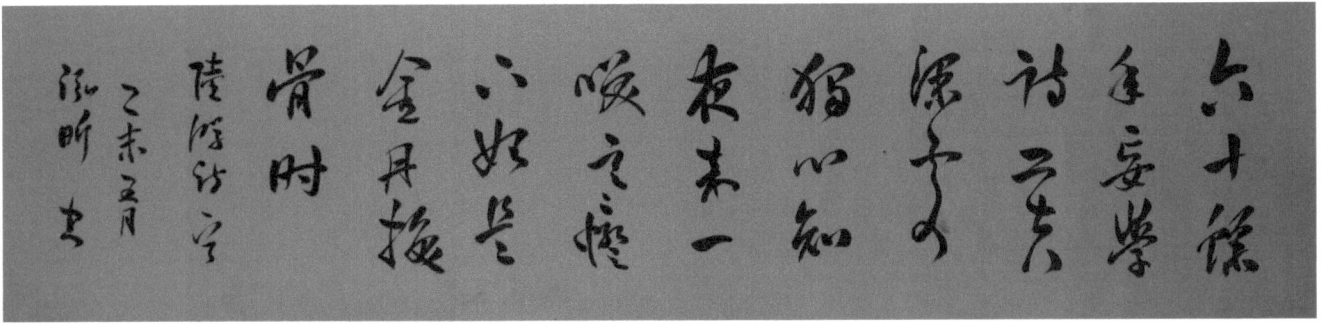

Voices of the Night, 2015

Part 3
PHOTOGRAPHY

Hong Kong, 2018

Hong Kong, 2018

Hong Kong, 2018

Hong Kong, 2018

Hong Kong, 2018

Hong Kong, 2018

Hong Kong, 2018

Hong Kong, 2018

A Girl in Millions of Colors

Hong Kong, 2018

Hong Kong, 2018

Hong Kong, 2018

Qingdao, 2018

Qingdao, 2018

Qingdao, 2018

Qingdao, 2018

Qingdao, 2018

Qingdao, 2018

Qingdao, 2018

Qingdao, 2018

Qingdao, 2018

Qingdao, 2018

Qingdao, 2018

Qingdao, 2018

Qingdao, 2018

Qingdao, 2018

Qingdao, 2018

Qingdao, 2018

Los Angeles, 2018

Los Angeles, 2018

Los Angeles, 2018

Los Angeles, 2018

Los Angeles, 2018

Los Angeles, 2018

Los Angeles, 2018

Part 4
HONGXIN SONG

A Girl in Millions of Colors

Photography by Yi Song, Gaomi, 2006

Photography by Yi Song, Alexandria, 2009

A Girl in Millions of Colors

Photography by Yi Song, Giza, 2009

Painting, Calligraphy and Photography by Hongxin Song

Photography by Yi Song, Luxor, 2009

A Girl in Millions of Colors

Photography by Yi Song, Istanbul, 2009

Painting, Calligraphy and Photography by Hongxin Song

Photography by Yemen Chen, Qingdao, 2010

Photography by Yi Song, Halong, 2010

Photography by Yi Song, Agra, 2013

Photography by Yi Song, Lalitpur, 2013

Painting, Calligraphy and Photography by Hongxin Song

Photography by Yemen Chen, Qingdao, 2015

A Girl in Millions of Colors

Photography by Yemen Chen, Qingdao, 2015

Painting, Calligraphy and Photography by Hongxin Song

Photography by Yemen Chen, Qingdao, 2015

A Girl in Millions of Colors

Photography by Yi Song, Acropolis of Athens, 2015

Photography by Yi Song, Roma, 2015

Photography by Yi Song, Venice, 2015

The Giant Panda Base in Wolong Nature Reserve, 2017

The Giant Panda Base in Wolong Nature Reserve, 2017

Hongxin Song

INTERESTS
Painting, Calligraphy, Piano, Guitar, Bamboo Flute, Tennis, Swimming, Taekwondo

VOLUNTEERING
Volunteer, "The Vibrant Future" International Education Project for Young Artists, International Society of Young Artists, Los Angeles, CA, USA, 2019 | Volunteer, Caring Stray Dogs, Qingdao, China, 2017-present | Volunteer, Community Public Welfare Class for Girls in Science, Qingdao, China, 2017 | Volunteer, Biological Big Data Research, Chinese Academy of Sciences, Beijing, China, 2017 | Volunteer, Wildness Training and Reintroduction of Giant Panda, Wolong National Nature Reserve, China, 2017

MEDIA REPORTS
Title: "Showing 'Millions of Colors' with Art", Subtitle: "Hongxin Song, a High School Girl from Qingdao, Publishes Pictorial Book in the US", p. 10, Qingdao Evening News, Qingdao, China, October 14, 2018 | Title: "Hongxin Song, a Middle School Girl from Qingdao, Publishes Pictorial Book in the US", p. B-7, Peninsula City News, Qingdao, China, October 17, 2018

PUBLICATIONS
Artist, *A Girl in Millions of Colors: Painting, Calligraphy and Photography by Hongxin Song*, 2nd Edition, Losget Press, Los Angeles, CA, USA, 2019 | Artist, *The Rising Young Artists from the East*, 1st Edition, Losget Press, Los Angeles, CA, USA, 2019 | Artist, *A Girl in Millions of Colors: Painting, Calligraphy and Photography by Hongxin Song*, 1st Edition, Losget Press, Los Angeles, CA, USA, 2018

AWARDS
Bronze Award for Art, "Award of Liberty" Annual Recognition of Year 2018, International Society of Young Artists, USA, 2018 | 2nd Prize, China Brain Bee Competition of Shaanxi, China, 2017

The publication of this book is part of a benevolent program - "The Vibrant Future" International Education Project for Young Artists, sponsored by the International Society of Young Artists. All of the earnings from the publication of this book will be donated to improve education for young artists.

LOSGET

Copyright © 2019 by Losget Press
All rights reserved.
Published in the United States by Losget Press, Los Angeles
Originally published in Paperback in the United States by Losget Press, in 2019
Names: Song, Hongxin, author.
Title: A Girl in Millions of Colors: Painting, Calligraphy and Photography by Hongxin Song / Hongxin Song.
Description: Second Edition. | Los Angeles: Losget Press, 2019.
Identifiers: ISBN-13: 978-1-7328459-5-4 | ISBN-10: 1-7328459-5-6 | eBookISBN-13: 978-1-7328459-4-7 | eBookISBN-10: 1-7328459-4-8
www.losget.com
E-mail: contact@losget.com
Book design by Tiger Hupo
First Printing. 2019.

www.ingramcontent.com/pod-product-compliance
Lightning Source LLC
Chambersburg PA
CBHW041452020526
44114CB00055B/86